Distance Education and Teacher Education at Armstrong Atlantic State University

by
Maryellen S. Cosgrove

ISBN 0-87367-640-8

Bloomington, Indiana

This fastback is sponsored by the Ohio State University Chapter of Phi Delta Kappa International, which made a generous contribution toward publication costs.

The chapter sponsors this fastback to honor Barbara Trent, secretary and treasurer of the Ohio State University Chapter, in gratitude for her constant participation and service in chapter activities. She serves as our model of a person dedicated to service, and she is our constant guide in responsibly planning and carrying out programs.

Table of Contents

Introduction

What do teachers, or prospective teachers, envision when they hear the word *telecommunications*? CEOs meeting in board rooms connected by satellite? Or students watching their teacher, who is miles away, on a television monitor? Both are appropriate.

Distance education — sometimes called "distance learning" or "distance teaching" — enables geographically separated individuals to interact and to learn. And the technologies of distance education are beginning to affect teacher education.

Consider the following scenario:

You are a professor of education. You enter your campus office and find a faxed lesson plan from Sally Smith, a student teacher now working in a fifth-grade classroom in a professional development school across town. You note that the lesson plan involves considerable student discussion, which has been a weak point for Sally. You e-mail a message to Sally, asking her to get in touch as soon as possible.

Minutes later, you are engaging in a conference with Sally and her supervising teacher by means of a two-way audio-video link. As a result of the conference, Sally realizes that she needs to incorporate a cooperative learning strategy in her lesson.

As you are winding down the conference with Sally and her supervising teacher, Dick Jones, another student teacher, enters the distance education room at the professional development school. Dick is preparing to teach a first-grade math lesson in the distance education room.

You invite a colleague from the college math department to sit in on your real-time video observation. As Dick begins his lesson, it becomes clear that he is having difficulty using an anticipatory set strategy. You activate a microphone connected to an earphone in Dick's ear and talk him through the strategy. None of Dick's students are aware of the help he is receiving as he works with them.

Later that day you model a writing process workshop for your reading methods students. Your class is scheduled to coincide with a fourth-grade reading class taught by John King, a veteran teacher at the professional development school across town. To show your students a writing process workshop in action, you activate the audio-video link between your classroom and Mr. King's. Your students observe the lesson. When Mr. King's class ends, he dismisses his fourth-graders and then turns to the camera and responds to questions from your students.

This scenario may seem like a day in the future, but it is happening now in the College of Education at Armstrong Atlantic State University in Savannah, Georgia. And it is happening — and can and will happen — in more and more colleges and universities each year.

In this fastback I will describe some of the key technologies of distance education in the context of teacher education at Armstrong Atlantic. The technologies permit college-to-school and school-to-school links, cross-cultural communication, and other expanded forms of communication. I also will attempt to incorporate some of the lessons we have learned in developing distance education at Armstrong Atlantic. My hope is that our experience can inspire and guide others interested in distance education and teacher education.

The Armstrong Atlantic program has received financial support from AACTE/Philip Morris, Coca-Cola, and the Georgia Board of Regents in addition to funding from the university.

Rationale

After more than three decades of teaching, I still remember vividly the instructional technology course that I took as an undergraduate. Our "state of the art" technologies were the mimeograph machine and the overhead projector. I also remember the instructor telling the class that those technologies probably would become obsolete during our careers and that we needed to learn to adapt and not fear the "machines" of teaching. Indeed.

Today's future teachers, even more than those of past generations, need to be ready to embrace rapidly changing technologies. Thus the Armstrong Atlantic program is not merely an experience in distance education but a philosophical introduction to the use of technology as a tool in teaching and learning.

In some respects distance education technologies now are permitting education to do what many businesses have been able to do for some time — communicate more effectively at a distance. College students on satellite campuses can now take the same quality courses as their peers on the main campus without having to commute. Educators from large regions can exchange ideas and concerns without having to lose valuable time driving to meetings. And high schools now can tap into college courses for their honors and advance placement students.

Excellence in education for *all* students is a primary concern in the Armstrong Atlantic program. In the past there were two distinct education regions in Georgia. One centered on metropolitan Atlanta, and the other encompassed the rural regions of northern and southern Georgia. If a school in a rural area lacked the resources or instructors to offer a course, then the students had to do without. But now the playing fields of urban and rural schools are being leveled by distance education technology. The distance education program in Georgia is not unique, but it may serve as a model for other states where distance education and teacher education are not yet linked.

Another factor that weighs in favor of distance education technologies is that such technologies are mirrored in the popular culture. Today's children are reared on MTV, video games, and the Internet. Traditional textbooks and chalkboards no longer meet the education needs of our children, and such "technology" no longer reflects the real world.

Moreover, today's students need to be able to cross cultural divides comfortably, something they cannot necessarily do in their own classrooms and schools. Distance education technologies permit and even encourage multicultural awareness and cross-cultural links. This aspect of distance education is consistent with Vygotsky's theory that students' learning is enhanced by engaging them in social interactions with others of mixed abilities and backgrounds.

The Armstrong Atlantic program provides direct experience with distance education for prospective teachers in two ways. First, students participate in interactive observations during methods courses. Second, students engage in hands-on experiences with distance education technologies as student teachers in two, geographically distinct professional development schools. These schools are White Bluff Elementary School in Savannah, an industrialized port city in Chatham County, and Dickerson Primary School in Vidalia, the county seat of rural Toombs County, which is known for producing peanuts, cotton, and, of course, Vidalia onions.

In addition to benefiting the prospective teachers, the Armstrong Atlantic program also serves the students of the two schools by linking them with one another. This link allows students in both schools to get acquainted with "virtual" classmates, children whom they probably will never meet in person. But as a result of the technological link, these students all come to know and better understand urban and rural cultures.

Distance Education Technologies

Armstrong Atlantic State University is a participant in the Georgia Statewide Academic and Medical System (GSAMS), which is the largest interactive distance education network in the world. In 1992 the Georgia legislature passed the Georgia Distance Learning and Telemedicine Act (SB 144) to establish a communications network linking public schools, state colleges, libraries, and medical facilities throughout the state. The Georgia model includes college students attending remote campuses, high school students receiving advanced courses, medical professionals learning about new procedures, educators conferencing with each other, and young students taking (virtual) "field trips" without leaving their schools. Thus far, more than 400 sites have been linked within the state, and another 1,700 are in the planning stage. Eventually the network will be expanded to include other states and countries.

The GSAMS network combines two-way, interactive, full-motion compressed video and audio transmitted through fiber-optic cables leased from Southern Bell. The use of compressed video and audio makes the transmission less costly because it reduces the electronic storage size of the transmitted images. The fiber optics are actually glass filaments, thinner than human hair, through which the compressed impulses are transmitted. The video and audio signals are converted into light impulses at one site and sent through the fiber optics at the speed of light before being converted back into video and audio signals at the other sites. All this occurs at 186,000 miles per second with 480 lines of resolution, thus achieving true television-like picture and sound quality.

Georgia provides each local site with a video codec, audio system, cameras, control system, monitors, graphic camera, video recorder, and even a fax machine. The video codec is the digital compression device. The audio system consists of the instructor's wireless (lavaliere or lapel) microphone, plus microphones hanging from the ceiling or placed on the tables so that the students can be heard at each site. GSAMS also has installed 15 voice-activated multipoint control units (MCU) so that multiple sites can be connected for a single class. The voice-activated MCUs automatically track on the image and voice of the last person to speak on the multipoint connection.

Two video cameras round out the transmission system. One is placed in the front of the classroom in order to view the students. The second is in the rear of the room, opposite the instructor's podium. The intent is for the instructor to look directly at the class, meaning both the students in the room and those in one or more distant classrooms. The instructor's desk is equipped with a user-friendly control system. With a gentle touch the instructor can move cameras to focus on one individual and zoom back to capture the entire room or operate a VCR.

Two large monitors in the front of the room permit students to see themselves and the students at the distant sites, thus permitting (and encouraging) face-to-face communication. A third monitor is placed in the back of the classroom so that the instructor can establish eye contact directly with the distant students.

A graphic camera, called an Elmo Visualizer, permits the instructor to display printed material on a monitor, similar to an overhead projector; however, the instructor need not make transparencies. Standard VHS player/recorders are included so that the instructor can show videos to students at each site or record a lesson for future use. A fax machine is included for the last-minute handouts and papers.

Because one of the purposes of the Armstrong Atlantic program is to give preservice teachers opportunities to conduct interactive observations from the campus site, a tiny ear audio receiver (similar to those used by television reporters) is included. The audio receiver allows a distant observer literally to whisper into the ear of the teacher at the distant site. An education professor or student colleague, for example, can coach the student teacher *as* he or she teaches, without disrupting the lesson. Although it takes time for the wearer to get used to listening while working, the audio receiver link to the college has improved many lessons by correcting misinformation and redirecting instruction.

The local sites have been responsible for renovating classrooms for electronic interaction. Major features are carpeting and insulation designed to control extraneous noise that can interfere with communications. Also, because compressed video images can appear slightly wavy, rooms have been painted light blue to absorb video "noise." Because any hanging lights might block a camera's view, all lighting has been recessed. Finally, acoustic panels have been installed in each corner of the distant education facility to absorb vibrations.

Experience has shown that a 16' x 20' room is ideal for transmission and the use of 35" monitors. If a larger room is needed to accommodate more students, then larger monitors also will need to be installed.

College-to-School Links

Teacher educators have long questioned the lack of practicing teachers' input into teacher education programs at the methods-course level. Goodlad refers to this phenomena as a "disjuncture" between theory and practice. Distance education technology now offers methods instructors the opportunity to bridge the gap between college learning and school teaching.

Observations in "real" classrooms usually create scheduling problems, disrupt the visited classes, and fail to focus on the important details of effective teaching. By using distance learning technologies, future teachers can become competent observers right in their methods classrooms and without disrupting the "visited" classes. What's more, the preservice teachers can "visit" far more classrooms using technological links than they can visit in person. And a follow-up visit between the observers and the teacher in the remote class also can be arranged. (Often another teacher or a paraprofessional can work with the students, so that the teacher and the distant observers can discuss the lesson, again using two-way audio-video.)

Because many preservice teachers' questions center on noncurricular questions, such as discipline, remote observation can be particularly useful. Students observed in person are more affected by the stranger's presence than students who are unobtrusively observed by a camera. Thus observers gain a truer sense of actual classroom management issues.

Close collaboration between practicing teachers and college education faculty was slow to develop. Although the relationship between the professional development schools and the college had been professional, equitable, even collegial, we rarely invited the teachers to become part of our courses at the university. As in the traditional model, we taught the methods courses and the teachers in the field provided a space for the preservice practicums. Therefore, when we invited the teachers not only to demonstrate "real" teaching but to do so on interactive television, they were understandably reluctant.

The first strategy to overcome this reluctance was to invite the teachers and their classes on virtual field trips to the university campus and other sites, including the Atlanta Zoo, whose instructors have refined distance education. This strategy helped both teachers and students to become comfortable with cameras and monitors. When the teachers were comfortable with talking to others by way of audio and video links, they were invited to participate in remote-link panel discussions during "Introduction to Education" and language arts courses at the university.

Next came reading aloud to students in a children's literature course, with the students, naturally, being in other schools and other classrooms. The "prop" of a book to read raised the comfort level, as did participating with colleagues in this new endeavor. Finally, the teachers were ready to move into demonstration teaching and follow-up discussions. When we got to this point, we asked for volunteers and were gratified when almost the entire faculty of each of the professional development schools raised their hands.

The next phase in our distance education partnership was much easier to implement: observation of practicum and student teachers. Field experiences traditionally are considered an important component in the preparation of teachers; and frequent, ongoing supervision with specific, constructive feedback is essential. However, practitioners question the disconnection in the traditional model. Once "placed" in schools, preservice teachers quickly become isolated from the university faculty. The methods instructors rarely supervise preservice teachers, and so links between theory and practice rarely are made. Research suggests that preservice teachers often forget their campus-based learning, simply adapting to the school milieu rather than consciously bringing to bear the instructional strategies they have learned.

Because preservice teachers in the field and their college supervisors are physically separated, often by several miles, it is difficult for the college supervisors to spend more than token time in observation and consultation. Distance education technologies can make observation more frequent by supplementing face-to-face observation with audio-video observation. And such technologies also make it easier to involve supervision teachers on site, thus enriching the interaction between college and school as well.

Our first opportunity to use distance education technologies to observe preservice teachers was during a pilot program for a new teacher observation instrument. As the student teacher taught a lesson, university faculty observed from the campus site. By turning off their microphones (linked to the student teacher's ear plug), they could discuss the lesson in progress without disturbing the student teacher. In this way we established inter-rater reliability of the instrument during the actual observation. This experience helped sell the College of Education faculty on the utility of distance education technologies.

Another goal of the teacher education program was to help preservice teachers team teach with both their student colleagues and experienced teachers at the professional development schools. Work on this goal had the serendipitous effect of moving both school and college faculty to network with colleagues in other schools and colleges across the state. Once comfortable with distance education technologies, most of the professionals were eager to expand their use.

School-to-School Links

The serendipitous effect of moving teachers to link with other teachers helped initiate school-to-school links using distance education technologies. The classroom of the future will include students who actually are sitting in other classrooms in the school, in other schools within the community, and in locations across the state or around the world. And teachers no longer will be dispensers of knowledge. Rather, they will become facilitators of learning, guiding students to connect with resources that come in many shapes and forms.

How can this vision of the future be actualized? In practice, most student teachers, once in the field experience, are disconnected not only from their campus-bound instructors but also from their student colleagues. Team teaching, with the difficulty of logistics and schedules, rarely happens among student teachers. But what if it could be made to happen?

In the team-teaching component of the Armstrong Atlantic program, student teachers are paired with other student teachers across the state to plan and teach lessons to their students using distance education technologies.

We began by meeting face-to-face with students to provide an overview about distance education technologies.

Next came an observation of an actual teaching demonstration — a remote lesson seen through technology. Students at several sites viewed the demonstration in real time and then discussed it over electronic links. This forum also allowed students to "play" with unfamiliar equipment and was part of the long-term strategy to help them become comfortable with the various forms of technology.

Once the students were formed into teams, they quickly adapted to communicating with one another in numerous ways, ranging from personal contacts and telephone calls to e-mail and faxes. Finally, the teams taught a lesson together, each student teacher teaching his or her own students, as well as the students in the remote classroom of his or her partner. Following this activity there were debriefing sessions that gave all of the student teachers time to reflect on and discuss their experiences.

Students quickly became aware of the constraints of the technologies, too. During planning sessions, the student teachers were mindful to avoid the "talking head syndrome" by planning activities to encourage active student involvement. And they wanted to involve students at both sites equally, which also took careful planning.

An offshoot (intentional on our part) was the encouragement of communication between the groups of students in the classrooms of the student teachers. By teaming their student teachers, we also teamed the children, who gained opportunities to (electronically) meet children across the state. For many children this was an initial cross-cultural experience. They were able to discuss their communities and lifestyles, in addition to the shared learning, which gave them opportunities to share writing and art, listen to literature and give book talks, and even sing together. And the children loved being linked!

"The Distance Learning Lab is great!" commented Stacy, a fourth-grader. "It's fun talking to people in different schools. The DL Lab connects people together. It is also a great place to learn and to have fun and to expand your mind."

"When I went to the Distance Learning Lab," said Louis, a fifth-grader, "we did different things. With my student teacher, we made things in there and shared them with other kids far away."

Although it turned out to be one of the best features of distance education during student teaching, coordinating the schedules for the team-teaching lesson proved to be one of the most challenging aspects of our partnership. The key, we found, was to nail down dates and times when the distance education classroom would be available *first*, then to work on scheduling the teaching times. Another strategy that helped smooth things out was for each team to select a leader who would be responsible for communicating about future meetings, sending materials, and keeping the college contact (me) involved in the process.

On several occasions, the teams chose the same day with back-to-back teaching — but to different classes of children. Although hectic, this proved to be beneficial because I required all of the student teachers to set aside that entire day and assist their peers with equipment and materials during their lessons. Consequently, during our post-teaching debriefing session, all of the student teachers were able to offer valuable input into each other's lesson. This process also created a supportive ethos for the student teachers, which lasted throughout their entire experience.

Another scheduling challenge was to match grades. This proved to be impossible, but it opened our eyes to the advantages of cross-age and cross-disciplinary teaming. For example, 15 student teachers were placed in prekindergarten through fifth grade at White Bluff Elementary School in Savannah, while only five student teachers were placed at Dickerson Primary School in kindergarten through second grade. So the ratio became three White Bluff teachers to one Dickerson teacher. When the third- through fifth-grade White Bluff students were involved, they actually became tutors for their Dickerson K-2 counterparts. All of this cross-age, cross-disciplinary pairing turned out to be quite beneficial to student teachers and children alike, because they learned that learning transcends the artificial barriers of grade and subject matter.

Cross-Cultural Links

Academic and social learning is strengthened when students actively connect their own lives with those of others. Child development theorists advocate that the learning and understanding of others begin with "self," then "family," followed by "community" before a "global" understanding can be internalized. Therefore, before children can become aware of other cultures, their knowledge and appreciation of their own culture and its relationship with others must be addressed.

Distance education technologies give us the tools by which children can meet other children from their own and other cultures — children with whom they can interact both socially and educationally. When such electronic meetings are complemented with multicultural content materials, cross-cultural awareness and understanding can be enhanced.

The team-teaching experiences that I described previously opened the door to cross-cultural student communication. Initial activities included students mailing one another letters, sometimes with photographs and self-portraits, or sending e-mail prior to a distance education activity. Another start-up activity was having the separate groups read the same multicultural literature before connecting electronically. Later, read-alouds in the context of distance education became a mainstay of the cross-cultural communication. For this reason, I will say more about the read-alouds.

Selecting the best books to enhance multicultural links among students is a key to the success of this endeavor. The literature must reflect experiences, emotions, and needs common to all. And it must accurately and sensitively address differences, such as their dress, diet, and social customs. In these ways the literature first can unite the students and then enrich their understanding of one another's cultures.

Read-aloud techniques also must be mastered by the teacher so that the reading holds the students' attention and reduces the distraction of the technology. In addition to using clear and lively speech, teachers who employ distance education technologies also need to follow sound practices that teachers use with all read-alouds. These practices include: using prereading strategies to connect the literature to the children's experiences, actively involving listeners at all sites by encouraging prediction and inviting students to join in for repetitive or rhyming passages, and using questions to monitor understanding during reading.

After-listening activities also are important. Students learn best by sharing and reflecting. They can extend the common listening experience by creating art, music, drama, or writing that draws on the themes in the literature. And, of course, the technologies exist to share these products, whether a discussion or a work of art, with students in classrooms far from their own.

With our mix of urban and rural students, it seems apt to categorize some of the following literature as Country-City. The other theme is simply Global. These books and the learning activities that accompany them are appropriate in grades K-5:

Country-City Literature

Bozzo, M.A. *Toby in the Country, Toby in the City*. New York: Greenwillow, 1982.

The two Toby's compare their houses, schools, and playtime. Extension: Rewrite the book using the names of students from the city and the country.

Burton, V.L. *The Little House*. Boston: Houghton Mifflin, 1942.

This book illustrates how a city grew up around a house. Extension: Interview a family member about changes in the neighborhood.

Cauley, L.B. *The Town Mouse and the Country Mouse*. New York: Putnam, 1984.

This classic tale tells a timeless story of different lifestyles. Extension: Write a letter inviting a student to spend a weekend in the city or the country. Describe the planned activities, too.

Hughes, L. "City." In *The Arrow Book of Poetry*, edited by A. McGovern. New York: Scholastic, 1985.

This poem describes the city from morning to dusk. Extension: Compare to Tresselt's book, *Wake Up, City*.

Jonas, A. *Round Trip*. New York: Scholastic, 1983.

Block print illustrations depict a story about a trip from the country to the city and then back home again. Extension: Create a block print map connecting the city to the country.

Kovalski, M. *The Wheels on the Bus*. New York: Dial, 1988.

An adaptation of the traditional song, this book is about a city family taking the bus downtown to go shopping. Extension: Draw a large class bus and fill in the windows with different scenes the students see when they ride on the school bus.

Levinson, R. *Country Dawn to Dusk*. New York: Dutton, 1992.

This book illustrates a typical day in a country boy's life. Extension: Compare the book to Tresselt's *Wake Up, City*.

Lorenz, L. *A Weekend in the Country*. Englewood Cliffs, N.J.: Prentice-Hall, 1985.

Pig and Duck, who live in the city, decide to visit their friend, Moose, who lives in the country, but transportation proves to be a problem. Extension: Brainstorm a variety of transportation modes that the students could use to visit each other.

O'Neill, M. *Fingers Are Always Bringing Me News*. New York: Doubleday, 1969.

This poem is about surfaces and textures found in the country. Extension: Create an exhibit of country and city artifacts.

Tresselt, A. *Wake Up, City*. New York: Lothrop, Lee, and Shepard, 1957.

Told by police officers as they walk their beat, the book describes a typical day in the city. Extension: Compare to Levinson's *Country Dawn to Dusk*.

Williams, S.A. *Working Cotton*. New York: Harcourt Brace Jovanovich, 1992.

The story of a farm family's life is told from dawn to dusk. Extension: Wear clothing depicting country and city jobs.

VanLaan, N. *People, People, Everywhere!* New York: Knopf, 1992.

This poem describes urban growth. Extension: Compare to Burton's *The Little House*.

Global-Theme Literature

Aliki. *We Are Best Friends*. New York: Dial, 1990.

Two boys keep their friendship alive by mailing pictures and letters to each other after one of the boys moves away. Extension: Mail a picture or letter to a friend. Using a map, mark all the locations to which students mail their letters.

Bagert, B. "Our Country's Quilt." In *Literature and the Child*, 3rd ed., edited by B.E. Cullinan and L. Galda. New York: Harcourt Brace Jovanovich, 1994.

This poem describes a quilt that depicts a variety of lifestyles. Extension: Compare the poem to Flournoy's book, *The Patchwork Quilt*.

Dooley, N. *Everybody Cooks Rice.* New York: Carolrhoda Press, 1991.

This story describes a multicultural neighborhood in which each family prepares rice in different kinds of meals (recipes included). Extension: Prepare the rice recipes and write a class cook book.

Flournoy, V. *The Patchwork Quilt.* New York: Dial, 1985.

A child and her grandmother sew a quilt made from scraps of the family's clothing. Extension: Make a class quilt and share it with another class.

Gray, N. *A Country Far Away.* New York: Orchard Books, 1988.

This book parallels the life of an African boy with a North American boy. Extension: Rewrite the book to personalize it.

Kellogg, S. *Island of the Skog.* New York: Dial Books, 1973.

Mice settlers on an island are terrorized by an unknown creature until they realize that it is a harmless "Skog". Extension: Using paper-bag puppets, reenact the story.

Kuklin, S. *How My Family Lives in America.* New York: Bradbury, 1992.

Three children from different cultures describe their daily routines and ethnic celebrations. The theme of food preparation is predominant throughout the book (recipes included). Extension: Prepare ethnic foods representing the diversity in the class.

Raynor, D. *My Friends Live in Many Places*. New York: Whitman, 1980.

Detailed photographs illustrate the commonality of different peoples throughout the world. Extension: Using family photographs, create a class book.

Sharmat, M.W. *Gila Monsters Meet You at the Airport*. New York: Puffin Books, 1980.

This book tells of misconceptions of life in another part of the United States. Extension: Draw a picture of life in your neighborhood.

Shelby, A. *Potluck*. New York: Orchard Press, 1991.

This alphabet book describes foods from around the world. Extension: Write a class cookbook of favorite family recipes.

Zolotow, C. *My Friend John*. New York: Harper & Row, 1968.

Two friends have very different customs and rules. Extension: Create a mobile comparing and contrasting the two friends.

As these few suggestions show, multicultural literature is a powerful tool for learning across the curriculum. Following are additional activities that make for effective distance education lessons because they also address the multicultural theme and create active opportunities for students (both near and far) to interact with and learn from each other:

Arts

- Identify the meanings of the various colors in the Kwanza celebration.

- Create artifacts from other cultures, such as weaving, masks, and pottery.
- Listen to music from different cultures.

Math

- Count money from other countries.
- Use objects from other cultures to make equivalent and nonequivalent sets or design graphs.
- Write word problems using multicultural concepts.

Science

- Investigate endangered species in other countries.
- Identify the habitats of animals.
- Write letters to people living in different climates.

Social Studies

- Identify the economy in other countries.
- Write reports about the history of or famous people from other countries.
- Create a community using cartons and boxes.

Teaching-Learning Links

In the beginning, distance education technologies were used largely to send out, electronically, lecture-style lessons for students in distant settings. Today's new complex of advanced technologies are erasing this limitation. One goal of education reform is the re-examination of the teaching-learning process, and distance education technologies are empowering theorists and practitioners alike to think in new ways.

I stated earlier in this fastback that one emphasis of the Armstrong Atlantic program is to treat technology as a tool — technologies as a whole workbench of tools. Technology, however fascinating, is not an end unto itself; it is a means to an end. With this in mind, when we debrief teachers, both soon-to-be and veteran, we ask them to reflect on the uses of distance education technologies as means to improve all teaching, not just teaching that involves distance.

Teachers tell us some important things. They say, for example, that they adopt as a basic premise the idea that students learn best when they are actively involved and held responsible for constructing new knowledge. And they also note that students most readily construct meaning through questioning, probing, and reflecting. Teachers in the Armstrong Atlantic program design lessons using cooperative learning, which engages students in sharing ideas and experiences.

Following is a short list of "essentials" for distance education that are equally applicable in a single, low-tech classroom:

- Carefully consider materials and strategies to be used — particularly if they are to be used at multiple sites. Teachers must ensure that handouts and materials are readily available.
- Ask students to introduce themselves to one another, within a classroom and across multiple classrooms. Teachers should refer to students by name, not location, in order to build a cohesive environment.
- Involve students from the beginning and build in variety. Teachers need to balance strategies: some quiet, some noisy; some individual, some group.
- Encourage interaction not just between teacher and student, but also student to student. Teachers can use cooperative learning strategies to keep students focused on a shared learning goal.
- Seek feedback. Teachers must continually check on students' understandings, particularly for students in remote sites whose visual and verbal cues of misunderstanding can be missed more easily.
- Direct questions to specific students, and redirect questions so that students can respond to one an-

other's questions. Teachers also need to remember that transmission lags will require them to increase the wait time for students to respond.

- Attend to summarization and closure. Technology can be overwhelming, and so teachers must continuously review key points and make closure specific. Student responses can be listed, edited, and reviewed using a graphics camera.
- Give consideration to appearance. From a technical point of view, light colors and conservative accessories tend to "read" better on monitors and thus are less distracting for students.
- Enunciate. While a certain casualness of speech can be forgiven in face-to-face teaching, a clear "virtual" presence demands attention to clear, firm speech that is well-paced. In lag-time situations this clarity is essential, as are deliberate gestures that help emphasize or clarify verbal information.
- Balance the visual presence of students. Teachers need to be certain that all students get on camera at some point so that they can see as well as hear one another.
- Use eye contact to keep distant learners involved. Teachers need to make an effort to look at the camera as a way of maintaining eye contact with learners in remote locations.

One final point is made by many teachers with experience in distance education: Have a backup plan. Communication technology is neither better nor worse than any "machine," and machines sometimes break down.

When one works with students and teachers, one quickly realizes the potential for linking teaching and learning in new and exciting ways, either using distance education technologies or extrapolating new face-to-face methods from such technologies. And I would be remiss not to put particular emphasis on excitement.

"I was so nervous at first, but then I forgot about the cameras and just focused on the children. Then it was easy!" wrote one teacher.

"I know that I will be a better teacher as a result of this experience," commented a preservice teacher.

"The future and its technology is not so frightening to me. I taught a distance education lesson and survived!" enthused another.

Today's teachers, soon-to-be and veteran alike, are discovering that technology need not determine content, need not *be* content, but indeed can be used as a vital tool to deliver content. Moreover, distance education technologies offer means to solve other problems, not least of which is helping students connect with and understand the many cultures of our nation and the world.

For those who have not yet discovered the fact that the teacher's role is changing, distance education technologies can open eyes. No longer can teachers view themselves — or allow their students to view them — as dispensers of knowledge. Rather, they must accept responsibility to be door-openers, facilitators of learning who can help students gain knowledge about themselves, others, and a world in which technology is omnipresent.

Resources

Albrektson, J.R. "Mentored Online Seminar: A Model for Graduate-Level Distance Learning." *T.H.E. Journal* 23, no. 3 (1995): 102-105.

Ball, J., and Crook, B. "Texas Facility Serves as a Hub for Distance Learning." *T.H.E. Journal* 22, no. 5 (1994): 64-68.

Boone, W.J. "Developing Distance Education Classroom." *T.H.E. Journal* 24, no. 1 (1996): 61-64.

Carlson, C.M., ed. *Teleconferencing and the Classroom of the Future*, vol. 1. Washington, D.C.: International Teleconferencing Association, Distance Learning Special Iinterest Group, 1993.

Clawson, B.N. "Two-Way Interactive A/V Applied to Supervision of Student Teachers." *T.H.E. Journal* 20, no. 11 (1993): 67-69.

Cohen, E. *Designing Group Work: Strategies for the Heterogeneous Classroom*. New York: Teachers College Press, 1987.

Duning, B.S.; VanKekerix, M.J.; and Zaborowski, L.M. *Reaching Learners Through Telecommunications*. San Francisco: Jossey-Bass, 1993.

Elliot, L. "Taking the Fast Lane on the Information Superhighway." *Teaching K-8* 26, no. 2 (1995): 34-39.

Fetterman, D.M. "Videoconferencing On-line: Enhancing Communication Over the Internet." *Educational Researcher* 25, no. 4 (1996): 23-27.

Fyock, J.J., and Sutphin, D. "Adult Supervision in the Distance Learning Classroom: Is It Necessary?" *T.H.E. Journal* 23, no. 4 (1995): 89-91.

Gellerman, E. "Teleconferencing Systems Facilitate Collaboration and Distance Learning." *T.H.E. Journal* 22, no. 3 (1994): 16.

Goodlad, J. *Teachers for Our Nation's Schools*. San Francisco: Jossey- Bass, 1990.

Gregory, J. "Evaluating Learning Technology." *Journal of Higher Education* (May/June 1990): 269.

Grimaldi, C. "Dig into Distance Learning." *Electronic Learning* 14, no. 6 (1995): 12-13.

GSAMS. *Distance Learning Training and Reference*. Atlanta: Georgia Department of Administrative Services Telecommunications, April 1994.

Hilty, E.B. "Teacher Education: What Is Good Teaching and How Do We Teach People to Be Good Teachers?" In *Thirteen Questions*, edited by J.L. Kincheloe and S.R. Steinberg. New York: Peter Lang, 1993.

Howley, G.B., and Howley, A. "The Power of Babble: Technology and Rural Education." *Phi Delta Kappan* 77 (October 1995): 126-31.

Hunter, B. "Linking for Learning: Computer-and-Communication Network Support for Nationwide Innovation in Education." *Journal of Science Education and Technology* (1992): 23-33.

Johnson, D., and Johnson, R. *Learning Together and Alone: Cooperative, Competitive, and Individualistic*. Englewood Cliffs, N.J.: Prentice-Hall, 1987.

Johnson, D.; Johnson, R.; and Holubec, E. *Cooperative Learning in the Classroom*. Edina, Minn.: Interaction, 1990.

Knapczyk, D.R. "A Distance Learning Approach to In-Service Training." *EMI* 30 (1994): 98-100.

LeBaron, J.F., and Bragg, C.A. "Practicing What We Preach: Creating Distance Education Models to Prepare Teachers for the Twenty-First Century." *American Journal of Distance Education* 8, no. 1 (1994): 5-19.

LePage, D. "Distance Learning Complements a Pre-Service Mathematics Education Model." *T.H.E. Journal* 24, no. 1 (1996): 65-67.

Lowery, B.R., and Barnes, F.M. "Partnering to Establish a Distance Learning Program that Is Responsive to Needs." *T.H.E. Journal* 23, no. 7 (1996): 91-95.

Martin, B.L. "Using Distance Educational Design to Teach Instructed Design to Preservice Teachers." *Educational Technology* (March 1994): 49-55.

McCollum, T. "Georgia Launches Distance Learning Network." *Atlanta Computer Currents* (January 1994): 68-69.

McDevitt, M.A. "A Virtual View: Classroom Observation at a Distance." *Journal of Teacher Education* 47 (1996): 191-95.

McLuhan, M. *Understanding Media: The Extensions of Man*. New York: McGraw-Hill, 1964.

Merkley, D., and Hoy, M.P. "Teacher-on-Television: A New Mode of Preservice Classroom Observation." *Phi Delta Kappan* 66 (January 1985): 373-74.

Merrion, M. "Theater Instruction Via Interactive Television." *Phi Delta Kappan* 74 (December 1992): 338-40.

Monk, D.D. *Using Technology to Improve the Curriculum of Small Rural Schools*. 1989. ERIC ED 308 056.

Moore, M.G., and Thompson, M.M. *The Effects of Distance Learning: A Summary of the Literature*. University Park: Pennsylvania State University, American Center for the Study of Education, 1990.

Parker, L. "Teletraining Institute: Uniquely Serving the Needs of Distance Education." *T.H.E. Journal* 21, no. 9 (1994): 30-32.

Rees, F., and Safford, B.R. "Iowa's Approach to Distance Learning." *T.H.E. Journal* 22 (1995): 63-66.

Riedl, R., and Carroll, S. "Impact North Carolina: 21st Century Education." *T.H.E. Journal* 20, no. 15 (1993): 85-88.

Rutherford, L.H., and Grana, S. "Fully Activating Interactive TV: Creating a Blended Family." *T.H.E. Journal* 22, no. 3 (1994): 86-90.

Schlagal, B.; Trathen, W.; and Blanton, W. "Structuring Telecommunications to Create Instructional Conversations About Student Teaching." *Journal of Teacher Education* 47, no. 3 (1996): 175-83.

Schure, A. "Towards a New Distance Learning University." *T.H.E. Journal* 21, no. 8 (1994): 32-34.

Slavin, R. *Cooperative Learning*. New York: Longman, 1983.

Slavin, R. "Cooperative Learning and the Cooperative School." *Educational Leadership* 45 (1987): 7-13.

U.S. Congress. *Linking for Learning with New Courses for Education*. OTA-SET-430. Washington, D.C.: U.S. Government Printing Office, 1989.

Verduin, J.R., and Clark, T.A. *Distance Education: The Foundations of Effective Practice*. San Francisco: Jossey-Bass, 1995.

Vygotsky, L.D. *Mind in Society*. Cambridge, Mass.: Harvard University Press, 1978.

Walsh, J., and Reese, B. "Distance Learning's Growing Reach." *T.H.E. Journal* 23, no. 1 (1995): 58-62.

Whitaker, G.E. "First-hand Observations on Tele-course Teaching." *T.H.E. Journal* 23, no. 1 (1995): 65-68.

Willis, B. *Distance Education: A Practical Guide*. Englewood Cliffs, N.J.: Educational Technology Publications, 1993.